NOTHING BUT LIMERICKS

Compiled by

ALAN SYMONS

Polo Publishing-London

First published in Great Britain in 1998 by Polo Publishing,
P.O. Box 108, Hampton, Middx: TW12 3QJ. FAX: 0181 979
9425.

Copyright text: © Polo Publishing
Copywright Illustrations: © Tony Maher

A catalogue record for this title is available from the British
Library

ISBN 0-9523751-2-5

Printed and bound in Great Britain by
Cox & Wyman Ltd, Reading, Berks.

INTRODUCTION

The limerick is humorous verse. It is also a story in five lines. A story that has no generalities, is often ribald; hopefully witty, downright funny or clever. Many famous writers have indulged in writing limericks. Notably Edward Lear, although W.S. Gilbert, of Gilbert and Sullivan fame, was most adept at this type of poetry and indeed *The Sorcerer (1877),* with music by Sullivan, has the well loved limerick song therein:

My name is John Wellington Wells,
I'm a dealer in magic and spells,
   In blessings and curses,
   And ever-fill'd purses,
In prophecies, witches and knells.

The structure of the limerick is strictly ordered. There is a definitive pattern consisting of five anapaestic lines; and these lines have a consistent rhyme order. Lines 1, 2 and 5 are longest and always rhyme. Lines 3 and 4 are shorter and they too rhyme with each other. A sort of a-a-b-b-a combination.

It would also appear that the limerick is peculiar to the English language. However, I have little doubt that if one digs a little deeper they probably do exist elsewhere; it is just they haven't entered the popular arena, as they have in English speaking countries.

Here you will find over 400 limericks. There are of course many more; thousands more. However, I have attempted to provide for all tastes; from the artfully witty to those bordering on the obscene. At all times my overwhelming purpose is to provide laughter, or at the very least, a snigger.

The sources of these published limericks are far too many to list. Suffice to say many friends and relations have given me their favourites, amongst these, Charlie Symons' efforts stand out. The support of Jenny, Gilly, Sue and Ronnie is particularly appreciated. A special 'thank you' to Tony Maher, for his design of the cover and his excellent humorous drawings, and an equal mention to Chris Adams, for his brilliant computer work. Thank you all.

Alan Symons,
London.

Said a gloomy young fellow called Fart,
"This name's bad enough for a start.
    But my snob of a Dad
    Makes it twice as bad,
With his ruddy Sir Mark Ffart-ffart, Bart."

A passionate lady named Fay,
Told friend Joe as he staggered away:
    "On the Passamaquoddy
    We consider it shoddy
    To stop after one little lay."

Lisped a limp-wristed cowboy named Fay;
"It's a hell of a place to be gay!
    I must, on these prairies,
    For the shortage of fairies
With the deer and the antelope play."

A young airline stewardess; Faye,
Has achieved liberation today.
    She screwed without quittin'
    From New York to Britain -
It's clear she has come a long way.

A man with venereal fear
Had intercourse in his wife's ear.
    She said, "I don't mind
    Except that I find,
When the telephone rings, I don't hear."

I, Caesar, when I learned of the fame
Of Cleopatra, I straightway laid claim.
    Ahead of my legions,
    I invaded her regions -
I saw, I conquered, I came.

The fastest draw of great fame
Kept his gun in his pants - what a shame.
    Cause he drew at High Noon,
    Pulled the trigger too soon.
"Wild Bill Hick" is now his new name.

I'm not really much of a fan
Of poems with no rhyme in their plan.
    But there's nothing that's worse
    Than to read someone's verse
And finding the lines do not scan.

Among Senators it is a fact,
That of sex there's no lack;
    What with Oregon's Packwood
    And Teddy he's good,
But you should have known Ted's brother, Jack!

The content of most TV fare
Is a source of scholastic despair,
    Brimful of tedium,
    And for this medium
Anything well done is rare.

A computer, to print out a fact,
Will divide, multiply, and subtract.
    But this output can be
    No more than debris,
If the input was short of exact.

In Summer he said she was fair,
In Autumn her charms were still there;
    But he said to his wife
    In the Winter of life,
'There's no Spring in your old derriere.'

A tiny young bookworm whose fare
Had been volumes of Pope and Jane Eyre.
    Was treated one day
    To a rare Rabelais,
And crawled off with damp underwear.

A strip-teaser up in Fall River,
Caused a sensitive fellow to quiver.
    The aesthetic vibration
    Brought soulful elation:
Besides, it was good for the liver.

A goddess capricious is Fame,
You may try to make noted your name,
    But she either rejects you
    Or cooly selects you
For laurels distinct from your aim.

At a coming out party in Feb,
A dyslexic servant's a celeb.
   He made his boss hot
   When he said he forgot,
To go upstairs and make the deb.

Said Plato: 'The things that we feel
Are not ontologically real.
   But just the excrescence
   Of numinous essence
Our senses can never reveal.'

When an obstinate fellow from Fife
Insisted on loving his wife,
   Denying obsessions
   And dreams and repressions,
The Freudians feared for his life.

In childhood it's easy to feel
The eternal suffusing the real,
   But as the beholder
   Gets steadily older,
It doesn't seem such a big deal.

No matter how grouchy you're feeling,
You'll find a smile more than less healing.
   It grows in a wreath
   All around the front teeth -
Thus preserving the face from congealing

A rapturous young fellatrix
One day was at work on five pricks,
    With an unholy cry
    She whipped out her glass eye:
'Tell the boys I can now take on six.'

    All hail to the naked female,
    Big of bust, round of rear, pretty tail!
      Her lack of resistance
      Keeps the race in existence;
    May our yen for her tail never fail.

There was an old fellow of Fife,
Who lived a lascivious life.
    When his organ was limp,
    Like an over-boned shrimp,
He brought what was left to his wife.

    I wonder how King Arthur felt,
    When one day Queen Guinevere knelt,
      Saying: 'Tell me, my pet,
      How did Lancelot get
    The key of my chastity belt.

A shapely young lady named Fern,
Puts out and is paid in return;
    "And my earnings," she said,
    "I conceal in my bed,
Since the ads say to save where you earn."

A shepherd named Henry Fitzhugh,
Said to his sweetheart, "It's true.
    Nothing is moister
    Than a lovely fresh oyster,
Unless, of course it is ewe."

Man's greatest inventions are few...
Though pundits are prone to rate two
    As vitally clever-
    The wheel and the lever-
More essential by far is the screw!

A guy with a girl in a Fiat,
Asked, 'Where on earth is my key at?'
    When he started to seek
    She let out a shriek:
'That's not where it's likely to be at!

When the clients are more than a few,
There's a savvy old madam named Drew
    Who'll establish a line
    By displaying a sign
That informs all arrivals: FUCK QUEUE.

There was a young lady named Flo
Whose lover was almighty slow.
    So they tried it all night
    Till he got it just right,
For practice makes pregnant, you know.

Little Jane and her brother had fiddled,
And she wept that, by God, she'd been diddled,
    For she found he'd a cock
    Where she, 'neath her frock,
Had only the hole where she tiddled.

A widow residing in Filey,
Esteemed her late husband so highly
    That in spite of the scandal
    Her umbrella handle,
Was made from his membrum virile.

'Strip,' Leofric said, 'and you'll find
I'll take off the tax I've in mind.'
    So Godiva, she streaked,
    And nobody peeked,
Except Peeping Tom, who went blind.

Goliath was known for ferocity,
An cxpert in every atrocity,
    But was knocked in a heap
    By a boy who kept sheep -
A victim of teenage precocity?

A pious young lady named Finnegan,
Would caution her friend, "Well you're in again,
    So time it just right
    Make it last through the night,
For I certainly don't want to sin again!

A student of nuclear fission,
Made a bomb with official permission.
　　But the earth disappeared
　　In the bang; it is feared,
Through an error in simple addition.

Since the girl couldn't type, she was fired,
Then explained how she'd came to be hired:
　　"The executive's dong
　　Being four inches long,
I thought shorthand alone was required."

A lady who didn't like flies
Managed to hide her surprise,
　　When she opened up one
　　And found it was fun.
Now she willingly widens her thighs.

A newspaper writer named Fling
Could make copy from most anything;
　　But the copy he wrote
　　Of a ten-dollar note
Was so good he is now in Sing Sing.

According to old Sigmund Freud,
Life is seldom so well enjoyed
　　As in human coition
　　In any position,
With the usual organs employed.

There was a young lady of Flint,
Who had a most horrible squint.
    She could scan the whole sky
    With her uppermost eye,
While the other was reading small print.

An accountant who practised in Fife
Made love to the corpse of his wife.
    "How would I know, Judge?
    She was cold, did not budge -
Just the same as she'd acted in life."

At the picnic we missed Jack and Flo,
And no one had seen the pair go.
    After what seemed like hours,
    They returned bearing flowers,
But we know where they went—Ho, ho, ho!

Though you paid me up front," hooker Flo,
Told her client, "I'm still due some dough.
    I felt, in gradations,
    Eleven pulsations,
And I quoted you ten bucks a throe."

Said a parson, addressing his flock:
'So-called Progress is in for a shock.
    We've intuitive proofs
    Of a Devil-with-hoofs -
Which will put back the clock before Locke.'

When Theocritus guarded his flock,
He piped in the shade of a rock.
It is said that his Muse
Was one of the ewes,
With a bum like a pink hollyhock.

As the elevator car left our floor,
Big Sue caught her tits in the door;
She yelled a good deal,
But had they been real,
She'd have yelled considerably more.

There was a young woman of Florence,
Who for kissing professed great abhorrence.
But when she'd been kissed
And found what she'd missed,
She cried till the tears came in torrents.

With his pecker stretched limp on the floor
And the wench still imploring for more,
He said, "Ten hours screwing
Has been my undoing—
I simply can't fuck anymore!"

A gnu newly neutered from flu,
Bid his bollox adieu feeling blue.
A lad saw the gnu sad,
Questioned why, said his dad,
"There is nothing, son, under the gnu."

There was a young lady of Florence
Who could not abide D. H. Lawrence.
    When invited by Frieda,
    To follow the leader,
She expressed what is best called abhorrence.

Concerning the bees and the flowers,
In the fields and the gardens and bowers.
    You will note at a glance
    That their ways of romance,
Haven't any resemblance to ours.

A flea and a fly in a flue,
Were imprisoned, so what could they do?
    Said the fly, 'Let us flee',
    Said the flea, 'Let us fly,'
So they flew through a flaw in the flue.

A tutor who tooted the flute
Tried to teach two tooters to toot.
    Said the two to the tutor:
    'Is it harder to toot, or
    To tutor two tooters to toot?'

A lady, while playing the flute,
Was thought to be rather astute.
    Her runs were not always
    As fluid as Galway's,
But her wiggle was wonderfully cute.

Imagine please - a butter fly.
Then, no matter how you try;
The imagery makes
With Spooner mistakes,
One you can't beat - a flutter by.

There was a young lady named Flynn
Who thought fornication a sin,
But when she was tight
It seemed quite all right,
So everyone plied her with gin.

'If you dream,' said the eminent Freud,
'Your Id is in doubt, or annoyed.
By neuroses complex
From suppression of sex,
So passions are best if enjoyed.'

Cassandra declining to follow
His amorous leanings, Apollo
Exceedingly miffed,
Allowed her the gift
Of predictions that no-one would swallow.

There was a young fellow named Fonda
Who was squeezed by a great anaconda;
Now he's only a smear,
With part of him here,
And the rest of him somewhere out yonder.

In the days of mild President Ford,
Decorum and calm were restored;
   He did nothing much hateful
   For which we were grateful,
And terribly, terribly bored.

The limerick's, admitted, a verse form
A terse form, a curse form, a hearse form.
   It may not be lyric
   And at best it's satyric,
And a whale of a tail in perverse form.

I'm getting deep lines on my forehead;
My face is becoming quite florid.
   I measure with dread
   My middle-aged spread;
I think growing old is quite horrid.

Said a Tripper: 'O joy to have found
Such a glory of sight and of sound!
   How our heart-strings are stirred
   By the song of a bird.
As we scatter our litter around!'

A reckless young man from Fort Blainy
Made love to a spinster named Janie.
   When his friends said, 'Oh dear,
   She's so old and so queer,'
He replied, 'but for me the day was so rainy!'

Her Weight-Watcher diet she found,
Was crooked because of the sound
    Of the glamorous ads,
    From dollar-wise lads
Who gained before she lost a pound.

There once was an old Forty-niner
Who chuckled that nothing was finer,
    Than a lady called Red
    Who would climb into bed,
When he promised to wine 'er and dine 'er

A publisher once went to France
In search of a tale of romance;
    A Parisian lady
    Told a story so shady,
That the publisher made an advance.

A reckless young lady of France
Had no qualms about taking a chance,
    But she thought it was crude
    To get screwed in the nude,
So she always went home with damp pants.

There was a young person named Frank,
Who was keen to manoeuvre a tank.
    But when given the chance
    Made directly for France,
And went rather too far, so he sank.

There was a young student called Fred,
Who was questioned on Descartes and said:
    'It's perfectly clear
    That I'm not really here,
For I haven't a thought in my head.'

A cannibal chief, name of Fred,
Complained to his cook, "You shithead!
    With feet it's OK
    To serve white or Rose,
But with buttocks you gotta serve red."

A nervous young fellow named Fred
Took a charming young widow to bed.
    When he'd diddled a while
    She remarked with a smile,
'I'm afraid it's all up in your head.'

There was a young fellow named French
Who was screwing his girl on a bench.
    His prick was so small
    It did no good at all;
His shortcomings offended the wench.

A quirky old gent, name of Freud,
Was, not without reason, annoyed
    That his concept of Id,
    And all that Id did,
Was so starkly and loosely employed.

Withdrawal, according to Freud,
Is a very good thing to avoid.
    If practised each day
    Your balls would decay,
To the size of a small adenoid.

To cross streets in London's a fright.
The end of your life is in sight.
    Your ass will be plastered
    By some Limey bastard,
Because you looked left and not right.

A glutted debauchee from Froome,
Lured beauteous maids to his room,
    Where, after he'd strip them,
    He'd generally whip them
With a bundle of twigs or a broom.

A frustrated nympho from Frome,
Told her boyfriend one night at her home.
    "If your penis stays dead
    You can hop out of bed,
Put your clothes all back on and GO HOME!"

At the zoo, all the wallabies frown;
Their habitat's dull grey and brown.
    Says their Irish designer,
    "Bold hues would be finer.
Me plan? Dye me kangaroo town!"

God brought perfect man to fruition,
But viewing the scraps with contrition,
    He collected the junk,
    And created the skunk,
The snake and the first politician.

    I used to think maths was no fun
    'Cause I couldn't see how it was done.
        Now Euler's my hero
        For I now see why 0
    I pi, = e +1.

A Chinese track layer named Fu
Gave up labouring for something quite new.
    He bought a guitar
    Said, "It's better by far,
To do Country and Eastern for you."

    Though clerical errors are fun,
    The bishops decree there are none,
        Or else they infer
        That if they occur,
    They must never be seen to be done.

Whenever the abbot craves fun,
He summons the same willing one:
    A hot-panties sister
    Who makes his dong blister!
She is known as his sine qua nun!

Said Wellington: 'What's the location
Of this battle I've won for the nation?,
     They replied, 'Waterloo.'
     He said: 'That'll do,
What a glorious name for a station.'

There was a young fellow named Fyfe
Whose marriage was ruined for life,
     For he had an aversion
     To every perversion
And only liked screwing his wife.
Well, one year the poor woman struck
And she wept, and she cursed at her luck,
     "Oh, where has it gotten us
     This goddamn monotonous
Fuck after fuck after fuck?"
But his efforts to poke her, assiduous,
Met a dense growth of hair most prodigious.
     Well, he thought he might dint her
     By waiting till winter,
But he found that she wasn't deciduous.
He went whoring to find satisfaction.
But with whores, though accomplished in action,
     He never could capture
     That fine fucking rapture,
For the thought of his wife was distraction.
She remarked, "When all joking is done,
What I honestly want is a son.
     I would like impregnation
     If not copulation,
But to wed and have neither's no fun."

If inside a circle a line
Hits the centre and goes spine to spine
    And the line's length is "d"
    The circumference will be
d times 3.14159.

        "Oh sweet mistress mine of Listowell,
        I love you with body and soul.
           If your teeth were your own,
           And your shape not a cone,
        I'd say you'd be nice, on the whole."

There was a young curate named Lloyd,
  Who was seldom, if ever, annoyed;
    Although you might poke him,
    You could never provoke him,
 His sang was so terribly froid.

A beach boy who loved to have fun
Kept screwing a girl in the sun.
    While his ass, being bare,
    Cooked to medium rare,
The girl kept exclaiming, "Well done!"

There was a young man from Ostend
Who went for a drink with a friend;
    They had a few jars
    With two boys in some bars,
And so each had a friend in the end.

There was a young lady of Lundy,
Began fresh affairs every Monday,
   Thus enlarging each week,
   Her erotic technique.
Whilst chastely abstaining each Sunday.

A rebuke by the Bishop of London
To his randy young dean, Dr John Donne;
   'In the Name, Sir, of God, peace,
   If you won't wear a cod-piece,
Don't preach with your fly-buttons undone.'

A thoughtful young bride of North Lyme,
Said, "Although sex is simply divine,
   As I told Aloysius,
   Between douches and dishes,
I'm in hot water most of the time."

The Sky's are a pitiful lot,
There's Chom, and there's Spas, and there's Trot,
   Trot chose the wrong lobby,
   Flunked out to Bobby,
And the structures of Chom are all rot.

Grins a fey Swedish groupie named Lynn,
'There are Nordics who may not get in,
   For a screw sometimes bores
   When it's Danish or Norse,
But I sure do put out for Finn!".

A twitchy young bitch named O'Brien
Sighed, "Joe, you just keep right on tryin'.
   I'll leave you my card
   And when it gets hard,
You wire me , or drop me a line.

The members of our great university
Display the most striking diversity;
   Some wise and some foolish,
   Some saintly, some ghoulish,
And some of the utmost perversity.

An accident really uncanny
Befell a respectable granny;
   She sat down in a chair
   While her false teeth were there,
And bit herself right in the fanny.

If letters "Dear John" should occur,
Do not think too harshly of her.
   Although love is gone,
   Instead of "Dear John",
The bitch could have written,"Dear Sir."

A Greek boy named Oedipus Rex,
Found a babe who exuded pure sex;
   'Till they both did discover,
   The wench was his mother;
Now they're both pathological wrecks.

A calculus fit to compute on,
White light, and a head to drop fruit on,
   A mind to absorb it,
   And soar into orbit-
That's all that it takes to be Newton.

A sensitive girl named O'Neill
Went on the fairground Big Wheel;
   When half way around
   She looked down at the ground,
And it cost her a two-dollar meal.

There was a young girl named O'Malley,
Who wanted to dance in the ballet.
   She got roars of applause
   When she kicked off her drawers,
But her hair and her bush didn't tally.

There was a young man from Ostend
Whose wife caught him fucking her friend.
   "It's no use, my duck
   Interrupting our fuck,
For I'm damned if I draw 'til I spend".

St. Valentine, I would not fart on;
His life you don't want me to start on,
   No stud, I'm afraid,
   The man never got laid;
He just walked around with a heart on.

There was a young fellow from Ongar,
Who had to be barred from the Conga.
    The heat of the dance
    Made his trousers advance,
As the Conga got longer and longer.

In Milan, a young dyke named Orsini
Served her lesbian friend a martini,
    Then suggestively said,
    "Let's have pasta in bed,"
Which, of course, meant cunni linguini.

There was a young maid from Ostend
Who swore she'd hold out to the end;
    But, alas, half way over
    From Calais to Dover,
She done what she didn't intend.

There was a young man from Ostend,
Who let his girl friend play with his end,
    She took hold of Rover
    And looked it all over,
When it did what she didn't intend.

A scandal involving an oyster
Sent the Countess of Clewes to a cloister.
    She preferred it in bed
    To the Count, so she said,
Being longer, and stronger, and moister.

The fabulous Wizard of Oz,
Retired from business becoz,
    What with up-to-date science
    To most of his clients,
He wasn't the Wizard he woz.

I'm not Irish, or so I've been told,
But I do dream of that pot of gold.
    But my hopes are forlorn
    When I wake in the morn,
It's hardly cold metal I hold.

A kindly old doctor named Grover
Once said, "I'm clearly in clover,
    Not being a fool
    I use my own tool,
Whenever I'm probing for ova".

I feel sorry for young Doctor Dow,
Our ladies won't go to him now,
    When examining the parts
    Of Mrs Ray Hartz,
He should have said "Hmm" and not "Wow!".

An unfortunate lady had piles
and the ugliest bottom for miles.
    But her surgeon took pity
    And made it quite pretty,
All dimples, and poutings, and smiles.

A young man, whose name we won't mention,
Had a transplant to lower his tension.
    At the beat of his heart
    He'd let out a fart,
And his penis would snap to attention.

        There once was a man from Kent,
        Whose prick was so long that it bent,
            To save him the trouble
            He put it in double,
        And instead of coming he went.

A shrewd stripper named Miss Isadore,
Became wealthy from stripping and more.
    Her sultry fan dance
    Made men come in their pants-
And she owned the one dry cleaning store.

        There once was a woman from Ealing,
        Who experienced a very odd feeling.
            She lay on her back
            Turned up her crack,
        And pissed all over the ceiling.

"So why are you calling; you creep,
It's Easter, I'm trying to sleep,
    So unless you're a rabbit
    With a great chocolate habit,
Leave your name at the sound of the bleep".

"Take off your clothes Mrs Skinner"
The doc had the eyes of a sinner.
 "We'll see what you've got,
 So don't be distraught."
"But doc, do you plan to buy dinner?"

In the land of the great Golden Gate,
Where a male picks a male for a mate.
 All the men's dicks
 Smell a whole lot like shit,
And they think a girl's pap not too great.

An amorous chap known as Morton,
Was arrested for stampin' and snortin',
 When released from his cell
 He was madder than hell,
For the season has passed for cavortin'.

Telepathic old alien Fred,
Was arrested on Mars, when he said;
 "It's a source of much mirth
 That a creature on earth,
To converse uses holes in his head."

A jolly old fellow named Hugh,
Was arrested for saying, "look, snoo!"
 "What's a snoo?" they would cry,
 And he'd always reply,
"Oh, nothing much; what's new with you?"

Pythagorus, rarely obtuse,
Was arrested for brainchild abuse.
   Claiming; squares on these mothers,
   Like cool, man; just covers
The one on the hypotenuse.

         Ampere, combing Volta's toupee,
         Was arrested ecstatic, they say.
         And wired to Watt;
           "I was shocked; I forgot,
         That Volta'd be ohm Faraday."

A brilliant young NASA technician,
Showed his wife an exciting position.
   She replied, "It's the top!
   Now if only you'd stop,
Yelling 5-4-3-2-1-ignition."

         If intercourse gives you thrombosis,
         While continence causes neurosis,
           I prefer to expire
           Fulfilling desire,
         Then live on in a state of psychosis.

Said a French maid, "Je suis trop tendre,
Vis a vis with the opposite genre.
   But some day mayhap,
   I will find a nice chap
Who'll instruct me in double-entendre".

There was a young man of Jaipur,
Whose cock was shot off in the war.
    So he painted his front,
    To resemble a stunt
And set himself up as a whore.

There was a young woman named Bright,
Whose speed was much faster than light.
    She set out one day
    In a relative way,
And returned on the previous night.

A Hollywood actor named Jake,
Went missing right after a take.
    The cast gathered round him
    The moment they found him,
Face down in Veronica Lake.

There once was a man from Great Britain,
Who interrupted two girls at their knitting.
    Said he with a sigh,
    'That park bench well, I
Painted it, right where you're sitting".

There once was a man called Gere
Whose ass grew exceedingly queer.
    He insisted on habits
    Involving white rabbits,
And a bird with a flexible gear.

There was a young hunter named Shepherd,
Who was eaten for lunch by a leopard.
   Said the leopard, " Egad
   You'd be tastier lad,
If you had been salted and peppered".

There once was a woman from Nod,
Who thought babies came from God.
   But it wasn't the Almighty
   Who lifted her nightie,
It was Roger the lodger the sod.

There once was a man called Dave,
Who kept a dead whore in a cave.
   He said, "I admit
   I'm a bit of a shit,
But think of the money I save".

An epicure dining at Crewe,
Found a very large bug in his stew.
   Said the waiter, "Don't shout,
   And wave it about,
The rest will be wanting one too".

There once was a man from Bel-Aire,
Who was screwing his girl on the stair.
   When the bannister broke
   He doubled his stroke,
And finished her off in mid-air.

There once was a Bishop of Clete,
Who decided to be indiscreet.
But after one round
To his horror he found,
You repeat, you repeat, you repeat.

There once was a man from Madras,
Whose balls were constructed from brass.
When jangled together
They played Stormy Weather,
And lightening shot out of his arse.

There was a young feller named Perkin,
Whose was always jerkin' his gherkin.
His father said, "Perkin,
Stop jerking your gherkin,
Your gherkin for ferkin not jerkin."

There once was man from Darjeeling,
Who got on a bus in West Ealing.
It said on the door,
'Do not spit on the floor'
So he leaned back and spat on the ceiling.

There once was a man from Nantucket,
Whose dick was so long he could suck it.
He said with a grin
As he wiped down his chin,
If my ear was a twat I would fuck it.

A pansy who lived in Khartoum,
Took a lesbian up to his room.
    And they argued all night,
    Over who had the right
To do what and with which and to whom.

A young girl was no good at tennis,
And her swimming was really a menace.
    She took pains to explain,
    'It depends how you train,
    I once was a street walker in Venice.'

There once was an old man from Esser,
Whose knowledge grew lesser and lesser.
    It at last grew so small
    He knew nothing at all,
And he's now a college professor.

There once was a lady from Hyde,
Who ate a green apple and died.
    Whilst her lover lamented
    The apple fermented,
    And made her cider inside.

There was a young lady one Fall,
Who wore a paper dress to a ball.
    The dress, it caught fire,
    And burnt her entire
Front page, sporting section and all.

There was a fat turkey called Sam,
Who gobbled whenever he ran.
He came out of the bush,
Wiggling his tush,
And was shot up the arse by a man.

A mouse in a room woke Miss Dowd,
Who was frightened and screamed very loud,
Then a happy thought hit her,
To scare off the critter,
She sat up in bed and meowed.

In days of old, when knights were bold,
And condoms weren't invented.
They tied their socks
Around their cocks,
And babies were prevented.

There once was a girl from Madras,
Who had a magnificent ass.
Not rounded and pink,
As you probably think,
It was grey, had long ears, and ate grass.

In days of old when knights were bold,
Before lavatories were invented,
They laid their load
Beside the road,
And walked away contented.

In days of old when knights were bold,
Before lavatories were invented,
   They laid their load
    Beside the road,
And walked away contented.

        I sat next to the Duchess at tea,
        It was just as I feared it would be.
          Her rumblings abdominal
           Were truly phenomenal,
        And everyone thought it was me.

There once was a man from Nantucket,
Whose finger got caught in a bucket.
    As he wailed and complained
    His distraught wife exclaimed;
"Don't go on dear so much, just suck it."

       There's a wealthy old man from Tabreeze,
       With a maudlin affection for fleas.
         He'd grin with delight
          When they'd scratch him and bite,
     That perverted old man from Tabreeze.

A conservative lady named Taber,
Had a date with her radical neighbour.
    They argued all night
    From the left to the right,
In the end though, he brought her to labour.

There was a young man in the choir,
Whose penis grew higher and higher.
　　Till it reached quite a height,
　　It was quite out of sight-
But of course, you know I'm a liar.

Mary had a little lamb,
Its' fleece was slightly grey,
It didn't have a father-
Just some borrowed DNA.
It had a sort of mother,
Though the ovum was on loan;
It was not so much a lambkin
As a little lamby clone.
And soon it had a fellow clone
And soon it had some more,
They followed Mary to school one day,
All crowding through the door.
It made the children laugh and sing-
The teachers found it droll,
There were too many lamby clones
For Mary to control.
No other could control the sheep,
Since their programme didn't vary
So the scientists resolved it all-
By simply cloning Mary.
But now they feel quite sheepish,
Those scientists, now so wary
The problems solved, but what to do
With Mary, Mary, Mary.

Said an ape as he swung by his tail,
to his offspring, both female and male;
   "From your offspring my dears,
    In a couple of years,
May evolve a professor at Yale".

      There was a young lady at Thaine,
      Who took down her pants on a train.
        But a handsome young porter, who
        Saw more than he oughter
      And asked her to do it again.

They will need a computer to tally,
All the cowboys who scouted our Sally.
   There are some on her mountains
   And some on her fountains,
And quite a few down in the valley.

      There was an old man from Terentum,
      Who gnashed his false teeth 'till he bent 'em.
        When they asked him the cost,
        Of what he had lost,
      He said, "I can't, I just simply rent 'em".

An old man from Texas called Tanners,
Was known for his very bad manners.
   When he noticed the start
   Of an imminent fart,
He'd announce it with bull-horns and banners.

An earnest young leftie named Tarique,
Black-balled, when put up for the Garrick.
    Observed with a groan,
    "These balls are my own
I consider such conduct barbaric."

There was an unscrupulous Tar,
Who met a sweet thing in a bar.
    To get to her quicker
    He plied her with liquor,
And now she's an unwedded Ma.

A forward musician, Lahar,
Had a habit of goosing his Ma.
    "Go pester your sister",
    She said as he kissed her,
"I have trouble enough with your Pa."

There was a young whore from Tashkent
Who managed an immoral tent.
    Day out and day in,
    She lay writhing in sin
Giving thanks, it was 6 months to Lent.

There once were two persons of taste,
Who were beautiful down to the waist,
    They made passionate love
    To the regions above,
And thus stayed reasonably chaste.

I sat next to the Duchess at tea,
She enquired, " Do you fart when you pee?",
   I replied with a snap,
   'Do you belch when you crap?',
Which I fancy was one up to me.

There was a young lady from Keele,
Who was raped in the lake by an eel.
   One morning at dawn
   She gave birth to a prawn,
Two crabs and a small river seal.

There was a young fellow named Ted,
Who had a radio put in his head.
   Long wave or short
   He did it for sport-
And to improve his reception in bed.

There once was a pirate, the story relates,
Who loved to go dancing on roller skates.
   But he fell on his cutlass
   Which rendered him nutless,
And made him quite useless on dates.

The puritans, living in Ealing,
Express all their horrors with feeling.
   Because the sight of a chair
   With all its' legs bare,
Make them look straight away at the ceiling.

In the back seat Marlene was a terror,
But taking the pill seemed to scare her.
     Said she, " Goodness sakes,
     I don't make mistakes",
In nine months, she gave birth to an error.

Oh God, for as much as without thee,
We are not enabled to doubt thee.
     Help us, by thy grace,
     For the whole human race,
We know nothing whatever about thee.

In the reign of King George the Third,
The fashionable shag was a bird.
     The hole of the sparrow
     Was dry, pink, and narrow,
And greased with Humming Bird's turd.

The spouse of a pretty young thing,
Came home from the wars in the Spring.
     He was lame,
     But he came, with his dame like a flame,
A discharge is a wonderful thing.

There was a young lady from Thrace,
Whose waist were too tight to lace.
     Her mother said, " Nelly,
     There's more in your belly,
Than ever went into your face."

The time is a quarter past three,
My wife's body's pressed against me.
   My desire, it is growing
    But she think's it's shamming
And moans, " Get out of bed and go pee".

        An indolent vicar of Bray
        His roses allowed to decay.
           His wife, more alert,
            Bought a powerful Flit squirt,
        And said to her spouse, "Let us spray".

There was a young man of Tibet,
And this is the strangest one yet.
   His prick was so long,
   So pointed, so strong,
He could bugger six Greeks en brochette.

        An old archaeologist named Throstle,
        Discovered a marvellous fossil.
           He knew from its' bend,
            And the knob on the end,
        It was the Hampton of Paul the Apostle.

There was a young lady of Flune,
Who was blocked by The Man in the Moon.
   Well, it's been great fun
   She remarked when he come
But I'm sorry you came quite so soon.

Said Orvil to Wilbour, " Hold tight,
We're going to make our first flight.
The ground we shall shift off,
Hurrah, we have lift off,"
And both of the brothers were Wright.

Said he," Please excuse my timidity,
It's just my God-damned frigidity".
But she sulked, "Oh my dear,
It would soon disappear
If your tool had some God-damned rigidity."

There was a young girl from Wembly,
Who was scared to go to assembly.
When asked simply why
She replied with a sigh,
"It makes me go all hot and trembly."

A progressive professor named Tithers,
Held classes each evening for sinners.
They were graded and spaced
So the very debased,
Would not be held back by weak sinners.

There once was a girl called Sophie,
Who won a lovely big trophy.
It was shiny with gold
It never was sold,
That lucky young girl named Sophie.

There was a young boy called Charlie,
Who never ate wheat but ate barley.
 The food, it was rough
 But it made the lad tough,
That lovely young boy called Charlie.

   There was a young poet of Theasus,
   Who went twilight walks with the Muses.
    But the nymphs of the air,
    Are not quite what they were
   And the practise has led to abuses.

Said a slant-eyed young jade from Japan,
"I must study under Gaugin",
 Though he taught her at first
 Soon their roles were reversed,
And she became Yin and he Yan.

   A lissom psychotic named Jane,
   Once sucked every man on a train.
    Said she, "Please don't panic,
    I'm just nymphomaniac,
   This wouldn't be fun were I sane."

An impish young fellow named James
Had a passion for idiot games.
 He lighted the hair
 Of his lady's affair,
And laughed as she peed through the flames.

A rather strange maid from Japan,
Spent most of the day in the can.
    Thinking thoughts Oriental
    Some vulgar some gentle,
And keeping it cool with her fan.

A peeker at peckers named Jay,
Hung out at the YMCA
    But the dick that he saw
    Was Detective McGraw,
Who hauled the piqued peeker away.

There was a young person from Leigh,
Who was neither a he or a she.
    "I think it's terrific
    To be non-specific
Gender-wise, don't you agree?"

There was a young man named Jesus
Who performed cheap abortions with tweezers.
    One night on the track
    Up a mummified crack,
He found a French letter of Caesar's.

He was giving the girl her first lesson,
Hoping head would become her obsession.
    But he pushed her away,
    Saying "That's not the way,
'Blow me', is just an expression"

There was a young plumber of Leigh,
Who was plumbing a wench by the sea.
    Said she, "Stop your plumbing
    There's somebody coming,"
Said the plumber, still plumbing, "It's me".

A highly aesthetic young Jew,
Had eyes of heavenly blue.
    The end of his willy
    Was shaped like a lily,
And his balls were too utterly two.

A wanton young mermaid named Jones,
Elicited undersea moans,
    From guys aqualunging
    By saltily tonguing
Their divers erogenous zones.

There once was a student of St. Johns,
Who wanted to bugger the swans.
    But the loyal hall porter
    Said, "Sir, take my daughter,
Them swans is reserved for the Dons".

A painter of pop-art named Jock,
Painted each canvas to shock,
    Outsize genitalia
    Gave his viewers heart failure,
But the critics just jeered, "Poppycock".

There was young student named Jones,
Who'd reduce any maiden to moans
    By his wonderful knowledge
    Acquired at King's College,
Of nineteen erogenous zones.

A renegade priest from Siberia
Whose morals were clearly inferior.
    Once did to a nun
    What he shouldn't have done,
And now she's a Mother Superior.

Says a showgirl who works at the Lido,
"I've accepted a flexible credo.
    I support women's rights,
    But there are frankly, nights
When the lib that I flaunt is libido."

At midnight Joe turned out the lights,
While she quickly slipped out of her tights.
    Then noisy bed squeaking
    Low moans, breathless speaking:
Thus man celebrates his sex rites.

As he struggled to heaven from limbo,
Dante murmured to Beatrice, his bimbo;
    " Sure, you want to scrimmage,
    But think of my image,
Don't lie with your pussy akimbo"

There was a young fellow from Poole,
Who found a red ring round his tool.
    He ran to the clinic,
    But the doctor, a cynic,
Said, " That's only lipstick, you fool."

        "My bride was no virgin." Said Braining,
        "I've never received such a draining!
            Mere up and down thrust
            Could be natural lust,
        But side to side action?, That's training".

A Magdalen Dean of Divinity,
Had a daughter who kept her virginity,
    The Fellows of Magdalen
    They must have been dawdling',
"T'would never have happened at Trinity".

        Said that luscious blonde lady of joy,
        Known in legend as Helen of Troy,
            "Having sex with Achilles
            Just gives me the willies,
        The Greek butters me up like a boy".

Two school kids around Aberystwyth,
Made love with the lips that they kissed with.
    But as they grew older
    They also grew bolder
Making love with the things that they pissed with.

When alone, a young woman named Julia,
Had qualities rather peculiar.
   And when men were about,
   Short, tall, lean or stout,
Her conduct was even unrulier.

To her lover, said pretty young Julie,
"I don't want to alarm you unduly
   I don't intend blame
   And yet, all the same,
You've produced a small pregnancy, truly."

Said Nelson, at his most la-di-da-di;
I'm sorry if I seem rather tardy
   But I face a dilemma-
   Should I bugger my Emma,
Or screw the delectable Hardy."

There once was a woman named Lana,
Who liked to give head in the sauna.
   The steam was so thick
   That she bit off a dick,
Now they call her the human piranha.

Said a cute university lass,
Who was taking a sex technique class.
   "How excited I am,
   Aced the written exam,
So now I've just orals to pass".

There once was a fellow named Lancelot,
Whose neighbours all looked on askance a lot.
    Whenever he'd pass
    A presentable lass,
The front of his pants would advance a lot.

Cried mother, "Why children, you're late.
You know I serve dinner at eight.
        So get into your seat,
        And be sure that you eat
Every carrot and pea on your plate."

There once was a fellow called Lear,
Whose verses were terribly drear,
    All except that
    With an owl and a cat,
Which is still quite a pleasure to hear.

A nurse once replied, with a laugh,
"You nerd", to a doc on the staff
        Who'd proposed with a whine,
        "If you don't sixty-nine,
I'd accept thirty four and a half."

There once was a golfer named Spear,
Who was sent to the clink for a year
    For an action obscene
    On the very first green,
Where a club sign read, 'Enter Course Here'.

When a randy old Abbess from Leeds,
Was discovered one day in the weeds
    Astride a young nun
    She said, "Christ this is fun,
And much better than fingering beads."

A harlot of note named Le Dux,
Would always charge eighty five bucks.
    But for that she would suck you,
    And wink-off and fuck you-
The whole thing was simply de luxe.

There once was a young lass of Leigh,
Who debauched on many a spree,
    Now she writes to the papers,
    Condemning such capers,
And signs herself,'Mother of Three'.

A careless young student from Leeds,
One day had to pay for misdeeds,
    When a man with a gun,
    Said, "You'll marry her, son:
You must harvest, when you sow the seeds".

A crazy old person from Leeds,
Rashly swallowed a packet of seeds,
    In a month his poor arse
    Was all covered with grass
And he couldn't sit down for the weeds.

She reacted, did novice whore Lee;
To her first fuck for dollars, with glee.
   She was bursting with pride:
   "I'm in business" she cried,
"Since a John has his business in me".

      A marriage advisor from Leeds,
      Said, " What your wife patently needs,
         Is husbandly passion
         In every known fashion,
      With a nice variation in speeds."

A myopic tree cutter named Lee,
Trapped an agile young girl in a tree.
   Jeered she, " Shift your whopper
   You careless tree lopper,
That's a moss covered knothole, not me."

      A reckless young sculler named Box,
      Forced the Oxford crew onto the rocks,
         The Eight shouted, "Rowlocks!,
         You've ripped out our bowlocks
      And terribly injured our cox".

A young Scotsman named Hamish O'Brown,
Offered a tart half a crown,
   "We Campbells," She cried,
   " Have still got our pride,
I'll not accept that lying down."

There was a shy virgin named Grace,
Who said, "If the whole human race.
    Depends upon what
    The boys call a twat,
Then it's put in a damn funny place".

There was a young lady named Joan,
Who went to the dentist alone.
    In a fit of depravity
    He filled the wrong cavity;
She nurses the filling at home.

There was a young girl of Kinsale
Who offered her body for sale.
    To be kind to the blind
    She engraved her behind,
With detailed instructions in Braille.

There was a young lady named Starkie
Who had a night out with a darkie,
    The result of her sins
    Was quads and not twins,
One black, one white and two khaki.

A policeman from Paddington Junction,
Whose organ had long ceased to function.
    All the days of her life
    Deceived his poor wife,
By the dexterous use of his truncheon.

There was a young Scottie named Coates,
Who wearied of living on groats,
　　For a change, in the end
　　He married a Friend,
And nightly enjoy's Quaker oats.

A major, with wonderful force,
Called out in Hyde Park for a horse.
　　All the keepers looked round,
　　But no horse could be found,
So he just rhododendron, of course.

There was a young lady named Grace,
Who had eyes in a very odd place.
　　She could sit on the hole
　　Of a mouse or a mole,
And stare the beast square in the face.

A Tory once driving his motor,
Ran over a Labourite voter.
　　'Thank goodness' he cried,
　　'He was on the wrong side,
So I don't blame myself one iota.'

When twins came, their father, Dann Dunn,
Gave Edward as name to each son.
　　When folks cried, 'Absurd!',
　　He replied, 'Aint you heard,
That two Eds are better than one?'

In his youth our old friend Boccaccio
Was wooing a girl on the patio.
　　When it came to the twat
　　She wasn't so hot,
But, boy, was she good at fellatio.

For sculpture that's really first class,
You need form, composition and mass.
　　To sculpt a good Venus,
　　Just leave off the penis,
And concentrate all on the ass.

At Harvard, a randy old dean,
Said, 'The funniest jokes are obscene.
　　To bowdlerise wit
　　Take the shit out of it,
Who wants a limerick clean?'

A lass on the island of Clear
Once knelt in the moonlight all bare.
　　She prayed to her God,
　　For a bit on the sod,
And a hippy boy answered her prayer.

The limerick's callous and crude,
It's morals upsettingly lewd.
　　It's not worth the reading
　　By those of good breeding,
It's designed for us vulgar and rude.

There once was a cad from near Croom,
Who lured a young girl to her doom.
    He not only seduced her,
    He robbed her and goosed her,
And left her to pay for the room.

        There was an old maid of Pitlochry,
        Whose morals were truly a mockery.
            For under her bed
            Was her lover instead,
        Of the usual porcelain crockery

What he asked for- a four letter word,
It badly frightened the virgin Miss Byrd.
    But gin and insistence
    Wore down her resistance,
The four-letter word then occurred.

        You may not believe me, and yet,
        Older women are the very best bet.
        They don't yell, tell or smell,
          And they screw hard as hell
        For it may be the last one they get.

The first time she saw a man nude,
Said a modest young lady named Wood:
    "I'm glad I'm the sex
    That's concave, not convex,
For I don't fancy things that protrude.'

A lonely old maid named Loretta,
Sent herself an anonymous letter.
Quoting Ellis on sex,
And Oedipus Rex,
She shouted, 'I already feel better.'

Two middle-aged ladies of Much Hadhem,
Went out for a walk, and it bored them.
As they made their way back,
A sex maniac
Leapt out from the woods, and ignored them.

There was a young lady named May,
Who never let chaps have their way.
But one brawny young spark
One night in the park......
Now she goes to the park every day.

There was an old maid from Duluth,
Who wept when she thought of her youth.
And the glorious chances
She missed at school dances,
And once in a telephone booth.

There was a young lady named Wilde,
Who kept herself undefiled
By thinking of Jesus,
Contagious diseases,
And the bother of having a child.

There was a young girl from Peru,
Who swore she never would screw:
    Except under stress
    Or forceful duress,
Such as: 'I'm ready. How about you?'

There was a young girl named Bianca,
Who slept whilst the ship lay at anchor.
    She awoke with dismay,
    When she heard the Mate say,
'Hoist up the top sheet and spanker!'

'Watch out!' warned a mother in France,
'Lest his hand reach the fuzz in your pants.
    If his other hot mit,
    Is massaging your tit,
Your maidenhead won't stand a chance.'

A boy scout was having his fill,
Of a brownies sweet charms up a hill.
    'We're prepared: Yes of course,'
    Said scout mistress Gorse,
'My girl guides are all on the pill.'

When her daughter got married in Bicester,
Her mother remarked as she kissed her,
    'That fellow you've won
    Is sure to be fun,
Since tea he's screwed me and your sister.'

Said an innocent girl name of Shelley,
As her man rolled her onto her belly;
   'This is not the position
   For human coition,
And why the petroleum jelly?'

Shed a tear for the WREN named McGinnis,
Who brought her career to a finis.
   She did not understand
   The sudden command,
To break out the Admiral's pinnace.

'It's Pony Express,' said Miss Pound,
'A wonderful game that I've found,
   Like Post Office,' she said,
   'But you play it in bed,
And there's a little more horsing around'.

There was a young lady named Mabel
Who liked to sprawl out on the table,
   Then cry to her man,
   'Stuff in all that you can-
Your bollocks as well, if you're able.'

A clergyman's bride, very chaste,
Who wanted a child in great haste,
   Said, ' Mother, I grieve,
   I shall never conceive,
I just cannot get used to the taste.'

Said the newly weds staying near Whitely,
'We turn out the electric light nightly,
　　It's best to embark
　　Upon sex in the dark,
The look of thing's so unsightly.'

Said a voice in the back of the car,
'Young man, I don't know who you are,
　　But allow me to state,
　　Though it might come too late,
I had not meant to come quite so far.'

A hesitant virgin named Mabel,
Remarked, ' Though I'm not sure that I'm able,
　　I am willing to try
　　So where shall I lie?,
On the bed, or the floor or the table?'

There was a young fellow named Fred,
Adept at getting girls into bed.
　　But best, by and large,
　　He much preferred Marge,
As Marge was so easy to spread.

A certain young actor, I'm not naming,
Asked an actress, he thought he was taming,
　　'Have you your maidenhead?'
　　'Don't be silly', she said,
'But I still have the box that it came in.'

On a date with a charming young bird
His erotic emotions were stirred.
   So with bold virile pluck,
    He enquired,' Do you fuck?'
She said ' Yes, but don't use that word.'

An observant man from Wales West,
Said, ' I've discovered, by personal test
   That men who make passes,
    At girls who wear glasses
Have just as much fun as the rest.'

Persuading shy virgins to sin,
Takes more that sweet-talking and gin.
   An all out seduction
   Is a major production.
It could take you days to get in.

When Carol was told about sex
She said, ' Mother, it sounds so complex.
   Do you mean you and father
   Went to all that bother,
And I'm just the after effects?'

She wasn't what one would call pretty,
And other girls offered her pity.
   But nobody guessed
   That her Wasserman test,
Involved half the men in the city.

The wife of an absent dragoon
Begged a soldier to grant her a boon;
    As she let down her drawers,
    She said, 'It's all yours-
I could deal with your whole damned platoon.'

Brigham Young was never a neuter,
A pansy, a fairy or fruitah.
    Where ten thousand virgins
    Succumbed to his urging's,
We now have the great state of Utah.

'Far dearer to me than my treasure,'
The heiress declared, ' Is my leisure.
    For then I can screw
    The whole Oxford crew-
They're slow, but that lengthens the pleasure.'

The French are a race among races,
They fuck in the funniest places.
    Any orifice handy,
    Is thought to be dandy;
Including the one in their faces.

Said a certain old earl I once knew,
'I've been struck from the names of Who's Who,
    All because I was found
    Lying nude on the ground,
With the housemaid, and very nice too.'

There was a young wife from Pretoria,
Who checked into the Waldorf-Astoria
Where she stayed for a week
With two Swedes and a Greek,
In a state of near total euphoria.

There was a gentleman named Charteris,
Put his hand where his young lady's garter is.
Said she, ' I don't mind,
And up higher you'll find,
The place where my fucker and farter is.'

My boy, if you like to have fun;
If you take all the girls one by one.
And when reaching four score
Still don't find it a bore,
Why then, you're a hero, my son.

While the Prof wrote a Latin declension,
His pupils did things one can't mention.
Like screwing and blowing
Each other, and showing
A singular lack of attention.

Said Queen Isabella of Spain,
'I like it now and again.
But I wish to explain
That by "now and again",
I mean now and again and again.'

Cleopatra, when sex was still new to her,
Kept buying up slaves to tutor her.
    But the Pharaoh, her dad,
    For fear she'd go bad,
Kept rendering then neuterer and neuterer.

There once was a woman called Mabel,
So ready, so willing, so able,
    And so full of spice
    She could name her own price;
Now Mabel's all wrapped up in sable.

A candid young lady named Tudor
Remarked to the chap who'd just screwed her,
    'After dildoes, dilators,
    And electric vibrators,
The real thing feels like an intruder.'

An Australian fellow named Menzies
By kissing sent girls into frenzies.
    But a virgin one night
    Crossed her legs in a fright,
And shattered his bifocal lenses.

Some night when you're drunk on Dutch Bols,
Try changing the usual roles.
    The backward position
    Is good for coition,
And offers the choice of two holes.

At Vasser sex isn't injurious
Though of love we are never penurious.
   Thanks to vulcanized aids,
   Though we may die old maids
At least we shall never die curious.

There was a young lady named Gay,
Who was asked to make love in the hay.
   She jumped at the chance
   And took off her pants,
She was tickled to try it that way.

There was a young girl, very sweet,
Who thought sailor's meat quite a treat.
   When she sat on their lap
   She unbuttoned the flap,
And always had plenty to eat.

Old Louis Quatorze was hot stuff.
He tired of the game, blind man's bluff;
   Upended his mistress,
   Kissed hers, while she kissed his,
And thus taught the world, soixante-neuf.

There was a young harlot from Kew
Who filled her vagina with glue.
   She said, with a grin,
   'If they pay to get in
They'll pay to get out of it to.'

A young window-cleaner, named Luigi
Was screwing a lady from Fiji.
   When she broke into sweat
   He said, 'Hold on, my pet,'
And squeezed off the sweat with his squeegee.

There once was a dentist named Sloane,
Who saw all his patients alone.
   In a fit of depravity
   He filled the wrong cavity,
And my! How his practise has grown.

In Wall Street a girl named Irene,
Made an offer somewhat obscene.
   She stripped herself bare
   And offered a share,
To Merrill Lynch, Pierce, Fenner and Beane.

A notorious whore named Miss Hearst
In the weakness of men is well-versed.
   Reads a sign over the head,
   Of her well rumpled bed;
'The customer always comes first.'

There was a young lady of Norwood,
Whose ways were provokingly forward.
   Her mother said, ' Dear,
   Please don't wriggle your rear
Like a trollop or tart or a whore would.'

A businesslike harlot named Draper
Once tried an unusual caper.
What makes is so nice
Was you got it half price,
If you brought in her ad from the paper.

There was a young girl of Botonger,
Used to bring herself off with a conger.
When asked how it feels
To be pleasured by eels,
She said, ' Just like a man, only longer.'

The lovers of kooky Miss Fay
Her neighbours believe are all gay,
For none, when they call,
Use her front door at all:
They always go in the back way.

It seems that all our perversions
Were known to the Meads and the Persians.
But the French and the Yanks
Earn our undying thanks,
For inventing some modernised versions.

There was a young man from Berlin
Whose prick was the size of a pin.
Said his girl, with a laugh,
As she fondled his shaft,
'Well, this won't be much of a sin.'

A yogi from far-off Beirut,
For women did not care a hoot.
   But his organ would stand
   In a manner quite grand,
When a snake-charmer played on his flute.

       Of my husband I do not ask much,
       Just an all mod. and con. little hutch.
         Bank account in my name
         With cheque book to same,
       Plus a small fee for fucking and such.

Sighed a newlywed damsel of Ealing,
'A honeymoon sounds so appealing,
   But for nearly two weeks
   I've heard only bed squeaks,
And seen nothing but cracks in the ceiling.'

There was an Italian named Julio
Who said, 'Sex is one thing I do know.
   A woman is fine,
   A man is divine,
But a sheep is numero uno.'

There was a young man named McNamiter
With a tool of prodigious diameter,
   But it wasn't the size,
   Gave the girls a surprise,
But his rhythm - iambic pentameter.

I love her in her evening gown,
I love her in her nightie;
   But when moonlight flits
   Between her tits,
Jesus Christ, Almighty.

In the Garden of Eden lay Adam,
Complacently stroking his madam.
   And great was his mirth,
   For he knew that on earth
There were only two balls- and he had 'em.

There was a young girl of Penzance
Who decided to take just one chance.
   She let herself go
   On the lap of her beau,
And now all her sisters are aunts.

When Lazarus came back from the dead,
He still couldn't function in bed.
   'What good's Resurrection
   Without an erection?'
Old Lazarus testily said.

There was a young lady of Wantage
Of whom the town clerk took advantage.
   Said the county surveyor.
   'Of course you must pay her;
You've altered the line of her frontage.'

There's a girl on Marathon Key
Who gave my mate, Len, the VD.
 Evil ways are a curse,
 Though, It might have been worse-
Had I called 'heads' it would have been me.'

   There was a young wife who begat
   Three husky boys, Nat, Pat and Tat.
    They all yelled for food,
    And a problem ensued
   When she found there was no tit for tat.

There once was a duchess named Sally
Who led her page up an alley.
 She was quite out of luck,
 For the lad wouldn't fuck,
And she muttered, ' How green was my valet.'

   There was a young woman from Chester,
   Who said to the man who undressed her;
    'I think you will find
    That it's better behind,
   The front is beginning to fester.

A round-the- world traveller named Ann
Took up with a Tokyo man.
 The relationship thrived
 And her baby arrived ,
With its' bottom stamped, MADE IN JAPAN.

There was a young lady at sea
Who complained that it hurt her to pee.
  'Indeed?' said the mate,
   'That accounts for the state
Of the captain, the purser and me.'

From the depths of the crypt at St. Giles
Came a scream that resounded for miles.
  Said the vicar, ' Good gracious,
   Has Father Ignatious
Forgotten the bishop has piles.'

On a picnic a Scot named McFee
Was stung in the balls by a bee.
  He made oodles of money
   By oozing pure honey,
Each time he attempted to pee.

Said the bishop one day to the abbot,
Whose instincts were just like a rabbit;
  'I know it's great fun
   To embrace a young nun,
But you mustn't get into the habit.'

There was a young girl from Sofia
Who succumbed to her lover's desire.
  She said, ' Sure it's a sin;
   But now that it's in,
Could you shove it a little bit higher?'

There was a young sailor from Brighton
Who remarked to his girl, ' You're a tight one.'
   She replied, ' Pon my soul,
   You're in the wrong hole;
There's plenty of room in the right one.'

        There was a young from Racine
        Who invented a fucking machine:
           Both concave and convex,
           It would fit either sex -
        And so perfectly simple to clean!

There was a young man from Australia
Who painted his arse like a dahlia.
   The colour was fine;
   Likewise the design.
But the perfume: Ah, that was a failure.

        A ballistical student named Raffity
        Went down to the Gentlemen's laffity;
           When the walls met his sight,
           He said: 'Newton was right.
        This must be the centre of graffity.'

King Richard, in one of his rages,
Forsook his good lady for ages,
   And rested in bed
   With a good book instead,
Or, preferably, one of the pages.

Said an old maid one fondly remembers,
"Now my days are quite clearly Septembers.
   All my fires have burned low,
   I'll admit that it's so,
But you still might have fun in the embers."

A widow who lived in Rangoon
Hung a rather large wreath on her womb;
   "It reminds me," she said,
   "Of my husband who's dead,
And how he got into his tomb."

A pass-throwing wizard named Reece
Prays nightly for marital peace.
   There are stadium cheers....
   There are bedchamber tears....
Both result from his famed quick release.

An ardent Scots lass in Rangoon
Went down on a Burmese quadroon.
   While the rising wind rasped
   Round the temple, she gasped,
"What a night for a blow! Come, mon-soon!"

Sigmund Freud says that one who reflects
Sees that sex has far-reaching effects,
   For bottled-up urges
   Come out in great surges,
In directions that no-one expects.

A comely young widow named Ransom
Was ravished three times in a hansom;
    When she cried out for more,
    A weak voice from the floor
Cried: 'Lady, I'm Simpson, not Samson!'

Henley's a special regatta,
Where the 'gels' have their annual natter,
    And puce-faced old chaps
    Wear striped blazers and caps,
And the rowing just doesn't matter.

So sweat your courgettes till they're dewy
(For l'eau is the foe of celui),
    While, golden in huile,
    As tomatoes you peel,
Your chopped onions fry free of ennui!

A hapless young golfer named Ray
Is involved with a frigid girl, Fay.
    A miserable linking
    Which drives him to drinking,
For she's an unplayable lay.

Said Oedipus Rex, growing red,
"Those head-shrinkers! Would they were dead!
    They make such a bother
    Because I love mother.
Perhaps should I love father instead?"

Said a young bridegroom boarding at Rye,
To his bride who was dreadfully shy:
    "Now that we're wed
    And together in bed,
If you can't, you can bloody well try!"

We all place a great deal of reliance
On the THEORY AND PRACTICE of science,
    But the hopeful intentions
    Of so many inventions,
Can be quite buggered up in appliance.

Said Calpurnia, 'Though I must render
Unto Caesar, the brunt of my gender,
    A few side effects
    Are permitted my sex,
When we're feeling illegally tender.'

A naked young tart named Roselle
Walked the streets while ringing a bell;
    When asked why she rang it
    She answered, 'God dang it!
Can't you see I have something to sell?'

There once was a girl from Revere,
So enormously large, oh my dear!
    Once out in the ocean
    Cousteau had the notion
To go down while in full scuba gear.

There was a young lady of Rhyll
In a bus was quite taken ill,
   So she called the conductor,
   Who got in and fucked her,
Which did her more good than a pill.

The hard-on of sheepherder Crews
Was one that he just couldn't lose.
   He'd no girls to assault,
   So perhaps one can't fault
His putting his dick to good ewes.

A concert conductor in Rio
Was seducing a lady named Cleo.
   As she took down her panties,
   He said, " No andantes;
I want it allegro con brio!"

There was a young lawyer named Rex
With diminutive organs of sex.
   When charged with exposure
   He said with composure,
"De minimis nor curat lex."

An unemployed teenage rhinoceros
Was arrested while swimming the Bosphorus.
   A hippo he'd dated
   Had announced: "We've created
The world's very first hippopoceros."

One midnight, old D.G. Rossetti
Remarked to Miss Sidall: 'Oh, Betty,
    I wish that you'd stop
    Shouting "Fuck me, you wop!"
It turna da tool to spaghetti!'

'Last night,' said a lassie named Ruth,
'In a long-distance telephone booth,
    I enjoyed the perfection
    Of an ideal connection -
I was screwed, if you must know the truth.'

A Manhattan cabbie named Rourke
Has a clever design on his dork:
    When he gives it a feel
    It expands to reveal,
An excellent map of New York

In Pinter's new play that's now running,
Our Harold's lost none of his cunning.
    Throughout the three acts,
    We hear just four facts,
But the pauses between are quite stunning.

Said a pupil of Einstein: 'It's rotten
To find I'd completely forgotten
    That by living so fast
    All my future's my past,
And I'm buried before I'm begotten.'

A psychiatrist fellow from Rye
Went to visit another close by,
    Who said, with a grin,
    As he welcomed him in:
'Hullo, Smith! You're all right! How am I?'

        There was a young lady of Rye
        With a shape like a capital I.
            When they said, 'It's too bad,'
            She learned how to pad;
        Which shows you that figures can lie.

I was sitting there, taking my ease,
And enjoying my Beaumes-de-Venise,
    With a charming young poppet,
    But she told me to stop it
As my fingers crept up past her knees.

        The food at McDonalds' a crime,
        A Big Mac ain't worth a dime.
            But if the needs are upon yer
            For a pee or a number,
        Their toilets are free and devine.

A stone knight in a chapel near Ealing,
Who had spent several centuries kneeling,
    Said, "Please keep off my ass
    When you're rubbing my brass—
It gives me a very strange feeling."

From the west to the fabulous east,
Lies the natural world - used to, at least;
   Look in forest or den,
   In zoo, farm or pen'
Now it's Man that is really the beast.

Since a top-heavy maiden from Yonkers
Is equipped to make tit men go bonkers,
   Poet Goldsmith might say,
   Were he living today,
That whenever she stoops, sir, she conquers

There was a young monarch called Ed,
Who took Mrs Simpson to bed;
   As they bounced up and down,
   He said: 'Bugger the crown!
We'll give it to Albert instead.'

There was an old person of Ely
Who spoke to his wife in Swahili;
   For as she could speak
   Only English and Greek,
He could use it to swear at her freely.

Eating is so elementary.
The food goes into the entry,
   The stomach, the gut,
   And heads for the butt,
And this is all alimentary.

Said Tebbitt: 'I don't understand 'em.
If they really want jobs, they can land 'em.
   If a work-seeking tyke
   Has no luck on a bike,
He can double his chance on a tandem.'

                The reason we're asked to endure
                A gutter press, smutty, impure,
                   Is that old river Fleet,
                     Whose name's on the street,
                Is an ordurous, underground sewer.

If you feel that you're right on your beam ends,
If your gait is more rolling than seamen's,
   And if camels in helmets
   March over the pelmets,
You've a touch of delirium tremens.

                'Oh, halt! cried Virginia, 'Enough!
                It's not that your beard is too rough.
                  Indeed, it's benign -
                   So close up to mine,
                But why not attempt the real stuff?'

Said an eminent, erudite ermine:
'There's one thing I cannot determine:
   When a dame wears my coat,
   She's a person of note -
When I wear it, I'm called only vermin.'

Said Einstein, "I have an equation,
Which some might call Rabelaisian:
   Let P be virginity,
   Approaching infinity,
And let U be a constant, persuasion.
Now, if P over U be inverted,
And the squareroot of U be inserted,
   X times over P,
   The result, Q.E.D.
Is a relative." Einstein asserted.

There was a young lady named Etta
Who fancied herself in a sweater;
   Three reasons she had:
   To keep warm was not bad,
But the other two reasons were better.

There was a young lady of Eton,
Whose figure had plenty of meat on.
   She said, 'Marry me, dear,
   And you'll find that my rear
Is a nice place to warm your cold feet on.

'Political women,' thought Yeats,
'Have come to be top of my hates.'
   His views rested on
   His love of Maud Gonne,
Who wouldn't go out on his dates.

Poor Hamlet! It's a fit to congeal ya,
To see what poor fate can deal ya.
   For what did him in,
   Was a prick in the skin,
When the prick should have been in Ophelia.

An old Danish jester named Yorick
Drank a gallon of pure panegoric;
   'My jokes have been dull.'
   He said, 'but my skull
Will one of these days be historic.'

Rupert Murdoch, filled with elation
At his newspaper's wide circulation,
   Said: 'With murder, divorces,
   And hints about horses,
I am moulding the mind of the Nation.'

They say that I was in my youth
Uncouth and ungainly, forsooth;
   I can only reply:
   ''Tis a lie! 'Tis a lie!
I was couth, I was perfectly couth.'

Prince Philip and Queen You-Know-Who
Were doing what married folk do,
   Cried the Queen, her heart drumming,
   "We're coming! We're coming!"
"How splendid," said Philip, "Us, too!"

A jolly young farmer from Yuma
Told an elephant joke to a puma;
   Now his skeleton lies
    Beneath hot western skies -
The puma had no sense of huma.

Hanging pictures," sighed clumsy Miss Young,
"Is a task that can make me unstrung.
   Thank God for my neighbour
   Who volunteered labour -
Both my pictures and he are well hung!"

Victoria said: 'We've no quarrel
With Shakespeare, but this is immoral!
   His Measure for Measure
   Incurs our displeasure;
We don't do such things at Balmoral.'

There was a young man from Ypres,
Who was shot in the prick by some snipers.
   The tunes that he played
   Through the holes that were made,
Were the envy of all the bagpipers.

It is clear that Napoleon's Queen
Was referring to army routine,
   When she said, in a flummox,
    'Marchons-nous sur nos stomachs?'
And was told, 'Not tonight, Josephine.'

A young lady sat on a quay,
Just as proper as proper could be.
    A young fellow goosed her,
    And roughly seduced her,
So she thanked him and went home for tea.

There was a young student of Queens
Who haunted the public latrines.
    He was heard in the john
    Saying "Bring me a don,
But spare me those dreary old deans."

A curious thing, the vagina,
Said a professor from North Carolina,
    It has lips that don't talk,
    And goes 'squish' when you walk,
But I've never seen anything fina!

A tenor who sang in Valletta
Was attacked as he left the theatre.
    Said the doc.: 'There's no doubt
    Paying Rudolf is out,
But he should make a smashing Musetta.'

There was a young lady called Valerie
Who started to count every calorie.
    Said her boss in disgust,
    'If you lose half your bust
Then you're worth only half of your salary.'

A desperate young lass from Vancouver
Liposuctioned her ass with a Hoover.
　　The massive reduction
　　Achieved by the suction,
Was generally thought to improve 'er.

Sighed the queen to a sheep-tending vassal,
Ere she sneaked her way back to the castle:
　　"Both my mouth and my quim
　　Will perform at your whim;
And, besides, handsome vassal, my ass'll!"

In History's Mysteries vast,
The present's as strange as the past,
　　But before you condemn,
　　Remember - pro tem -
You also are one of the cast.

Having rid Hamelin town of its vermin,
And been tricked by a noddy in ermine;
　　He lured girls and boys
　　With his pipe's pleasant noise.
Where they went, not a soul can determine.

There was a young lady named Gloria,
Who was had by Sir Gerald du Maurier.
　　And then by six men,
　　Sir Gerald again,
And the band of the Waldorf-Astoria.

There once was a girl from Versailles,
Who played with herself on the sly
    She started to come,
    And stuck in her thumb,
And said, "What a bad girl am I.

        Says an airlining wanton named Vi:
        "I'm a panty less stew when I fly.
           To a muffers delight,
           I'll take head on a flight,
        So the guy can have pie in the sky."

Sally-Jo was exceedingly vexed,
When they said she was quite oversexed.
    She said, "That's not true,
    I just like to screw.
Now, please take a number. Who's Next?"

Hitler, an extreme vegetarian
Looked down from his summit Bavarian;
    He said: 'It's not odd
    I'm superior to God,
For the latter is not even Aryan.'

A hurry-up hooker named Vickie
Was the quintescent queen of the quickie;
    She'd do a quick dance,
    Make you come in your pants,
Leaving you sullen and sticky!

I see a young lady named Kitty,
Lying down on the beach, oh so pretty.
To her boyfriend she blurts,
'Get it out please, it hurts,
You've lain in the sand, and it's gritty.'

He hated to sew, so young Ned
Rang the bell of his neighbour instead.
But her husband said, "Vi,
When you stiched his torn fly,
There was no need to bite off the thread".

After lunch the Grand Duchess of Teck
Observed, ' if you will listen one sec,
We've found a man's tool,
In the small swimming pool.
So would all of you gentlemen check?'

There was a young man from Belgravia,
Who cared neither for God nor his saviour,
He walked down the Strand
With his balls in his hand,
And was had up for indecent behaviour.

A deviate graduate from Trinity
Adored his sister to infinity.
Made a pass at his mother,
Had a thing with his brother,
And still got a first in Divinity.

A pious old lady from Worcester
Forgave all who'd ever abused her.
    But she flew into a rage,
    Which time couldn't assuage,
When she thought of one cad who'd refused her.

      There was a young lady named Sue,
      Who preferred a drink to a screw.
         But one leads to the other,
         And now she's a mother,
      Let Sue be a lesson to you.

There was a young lady from Hitchin
Who was scratching her crotch in the kitchen.
    Her mother said, 'Rose,
    It's the crabs I suppose.'
She said, 'Yes, and the buggers are itching.'

      There was a young lady of Devon
      Who was raped in the garden by seven
         High Anglican priests,
         Most lascivious beasts.
      Of such is the Kingdom of Heaven.

There was a young lecher named Trapp
Who thought using condoms was crap.
    Said he, 'Us real he-men,
    Like to scatter our semen.'
Six months later he still has the clap.

A Salvation lassie named Claire
Was having her first love affair.
    As she climbed into bed
    She reverently said,
"I wish to be opened with prayer."

There was a young girl from Mauritius,
Who said, 'That last bit was delicious.
    But if you don't mind,
    We'll postpone the next grind,
As that spot on your tool looks suspicious.'

There was a young girl of Bombay,
Who was put in the family way,
    By the mate of a lugger,
    An ignorant bugger,
Who always spelt cunt with a K.

There was a young lady from Maine
Who declared she'd a man on her brain.
    But you knew from the view
    Of her waist, as it grew,
It was not on her brain that he'd lain.

A plumber, who had a fine tool,
Was thought by his girl friend too cool.
    For when he was up her,
    He broke for a cuppa,
As that was his union rule.

Said an ovum one night to a sperm,
'You're a very attractive young germ.
    Come join me my sweet,
    Let our nuclei meet
And in nine months we'll both come to term.'

        Said a lecherous fellow named Shea,
        When his prick wouldn't rise for a lay,
            'You must seize it and squeeze it,
            And tease it and please it,
        For Rome wasn't built in a day.'

My sex life is pretty humdrum;
When I'm ready and want hubbie to plumb,
    He says, 'wait a minute,
    I've hardly got in it';
Then before I begin it, he's come.'

There was a young man from Calcutta
Who was heard in his beard to mutter,
    'If her Batholin glands
    Don't repond to my hands,
I'm afraid I shall have to use butter.'

Petunia, the prude of Mount Hood,
Devised an odd object of wood.
    Which, employed on hot nights,
    Gave her carnal delights
Far beyond what the average man could.

A fellow I know, name of Kimble,
Had a prick most exceedingly nimble.
   But so fragile and tender
   And dainty and slender,
He kept it encased in a thimble.

Said an unhappy female named Sears,
'The world seems just full of those queers.
   At parties I go to
   Are no men to say,"No" to;
They swish about, waggling their rears.'

Every time Lady Lowbodice swoons,
Her breasts pop out like balloons.
   But her butler stands by
   With hauteur in his eye,
And lifts them back with warm spoons.

A lady of features cherubic
Was famed for her area pubic.
   When they asked its size,
   She said with surprise,
'Are you speaking of square feet or cubic?'

There was a young man from Natal
And Sue was the name of his gal;
   He went out one day,
   For a rather long way
In fact right up Sue'z Canal.

'Active balls?' said an old man of Stoneham.
'I regret that I no longer own 'em;
   But I hasten to say
   They were good in their day;
De mortuis nil nisi bonum.

An octogenarian Jew,
To his wife remained steadfastly true.
   This was not from compunction,
   But due to dysfunction
Of his spermatic glands-nuts to you.

There was a young lawyer named Gorse.
Who fell madly in love with a horse.
   Said his wife, 'you rapscallion
   The horse is a stallion-
This constitutes grounds for divorce.'

     The toe of a postman from Dallas
     Developed a sizeable callous.
       His wife wistfully said,
       How she wished that, instead,
     It had been on the head of his phallus.

A young queer who was much oversexed
Was easily fretted and vexed.
   When out on a date,
   He hardly could wait
To say, 'Turn over bud, my turn next'

An Internet surfer named Fred,
Took a laptop computer to bed.
But we'll never know why,
For the poor little guy,
Tried to give his hard drive, some head.

To a whore, said cold Lady Dizzit,
'Lord D's a new man, since your visit.
As a rule, the damned fool
Can't erect his old tool.
You must have what it takes, but what is it?'

A bather, whose clothing was strewed
By winds that left her quite nude,
Saw a man come along
And, unless I'm quite wrong,
You expected this line to be rude.

Regardez-Vous Toulouse-Lautrec,
Though at first an ambulant wreck.
He could fuck once a week,
La Maniere antique,
And once in a while a La Grecque.

Said the Duchess of Alba to Goya,
'Paint some pictures to hang in my foyer'.
So he painted her twice,
In the nude to look nice,
And then in her clothes, to annoy her.

There's a wonderful family called Stein;
There's Gert and there's Ep and there's Ein.
    Gert's poems are bunk,
    Ep's statues are junk,
And no-one understands Ein.

There once was a vicar named Jake,
Who made the most awful mistake.
    He walked naked around,
    A grass covered mound,
And was bitten to death by a snake.

A Turk, named Abdullah ben Barum,
Had ninety five wives in his harem.
    When his favourite horse died,
    'Mighty Allah', he cried,
'Take a few of my wives; I can spare them.'

You will find by the banks of the Nile,
The haunts of the great crocodile.
    He will welcome you in
    With an innocent grin,
Which gives way to satisfied smile.

Did you here the bad news about Fred?
He took a bad hit on the head.
    But he didn't say Ouch!
    Or lie down on the couch,
He couldn't, you see, he was dead.